A Ministry of Caring
Participant's Workbook

A Skill Training Course for All Christians

by

Duane A. Ewers

with

Bishop Fritz Mutti

DISCIPLESHIP RESOURCES

PO BOX 340003 • NASHVILLE, TN 37203-0003

www.discipleshipresources.org

Fourth printing: 2008

ISBN 978-0-88177-289-0

Library of Congress Catalog Card Number 99-90318

DR289

TABLE OF CONTENTS

Introduction 1

Session 1: Theological Foundations for Caring 5
A Reading Resource — *Theological Foundations for Caring* 9

Session 2: Listening as Caring 13
A Reading Resource — *Listening as Caring* 17

Session 3: Speaking in Caring Ways 21
A Reading Resource — *Speaking in Caring Ways* 26

Session 4: Opportunities for Caring Contacts 29
A Reading Resource — *Making a Caring Contact* 32

Session 5: Caring for Persons Who Experience Divorce 35
A Reading Resource — *Caring for Persons Who
Experience Divorce* 39

Session 6: When Friends Lose Their Job 43
A Reading Resource — *The Unemployed/Underemployed
Worker and Caring* 46

Session 7: Caring for Persons Who Are Homebound 49
A Reading Resource — *The Experience of Being
an Older Person Who is Homebound* 53

Session 8: Illness and Caring 57
A Reading Resource — *Making a Caring Visit to the Sick* 60

Session 9: Caring for Persons Living with HIV/AIDS 63
A Reading Resource — *Caring Responses to Persons
Living with HIV/AIDS* 66

Session 10: Bereavement and Caring 69
A Reading Resource — *Being a Caring Person to
One Who is Bereaved* 72

Session 11: Adapting Caring Skills 75

Evaluation of *Ministry of Caring* Training 79

PREFACE TO THE REVISED EDITION

This edition of *A Ministry of Caring* has become necessary for several reasons.

First, I am more convinced than ever before that lay persons caring in their congregations and communities is a visible expression of God's caring for hurting persons. This is an expression of my commitment to encourage that caring to continue.

Second, there has been a rapid spread of HIV/AIDS and the staggering effects it is having on families, friends, congregations, and communities. I want to express my deep appreciation to Bishop Fritz Mutti, Topeka, Kansas, for writing the session on "Caring for Persons Living With HIV/AIDS." He writes out of his own family's experience of pain and hope. He writes as one who has been there — with grace, care, and sensitivity.

Third, I have personally experienced divorce, a new marriage, and the blending of a new family. The session on "Caring For Persons Who Experience Divorce," was revised to reflect some of my personal insights, especially as divorce affects children.

Finally this revision gives me an opportunity to improve the quality of the resource by giving clearer directions, expanding ideas, adding new insights gained from working with hundreds of lay persons and clergy, and updating the suggestions for additional readings.

Duane A. Ewers

INTRODUCTION

Objectives of a Ministry of Caring

A Ministry of Caring is a skill training course for individuals who desire to become more effective caregivers in their day-to-day contacts or for groups that have been recruited by the pastor or a program committee in the church for more organized caring. Detailed suggestions for the development of a ministry of caring are found in *A Ministry of Caring: Congregational Guide.*

The objectives of the course are to help participants:

1. affirm God's call to all Christians to care for hurting persons in order that they might have hope and experience growth towards wholeness;

2. become more sensitive to caring opportunities and be more intentional as caregivers in their day-to-day living within their families, among their co-workers, and within the church and community;

3. develop skills and insights that can be used for more effective caring; and

4. recognize their own need for, and learn to be receptive to, caring and support.

This course is not intended to develop paraprofessionals who will help the pastor do his or her work. The intention is to help participants become acquainted with caring skills for their own ministry that they might begin to practice and to further develop through later training and experience. The emphasis is on caring for people, not on curing them.

While the main emphasis of *A Ministry of Caring* is person-to-person caregiving, the course also gives some attention to the role of the community of faith in providing care for hurting persons.

Design of the Training Course

The course is a series of eleven sessions of one and one-half hours each with suggestions at the end of several sections for expanded sessions.

The first four sessions are designed to be basic and should be used before any of the last seven sessions. The intent is to use the insights and skills addressed in the first four sessions so that one might be a more effective caregiver to persons who experience one of the hurting situations described in sessions five through ten. Sessions five through ten do not build on one another so they do not need to be followed in sequence. As a group the decision might be made to focus on only one or two of those special concerns. The last session is designed so that the basic skills developed in the first four sessions might be utilized in caring for a person who has a hurt, struggle, or concern not addressed in any of these printed materials. Session eleven could serve as a guide for numerous sessions in a training or support group where participants would bring their own special concerns.

The material in this course has been used for over fifteen years to train laity for a caring ministry. It has been used and evaluated by groups in congregations and by clergy and laity who were trained to lead groups in their churches. It is an advanced course in a national lay speakers program. While ten to twelve persons is a good size group, the material has been used effectively, with some adaptations, in groups as small as eight and as large as seventy.

This course is designed in such a way that a pastor or lay person who is trained in a "helping profession," or a lay person who has received training from this or a similar course, may lead it.

The Participant's Workbook

The *Participant's Workbook* contains all of the material members of the group will need. Participants will be asked to record their experiences, insights, and reflections in the Workbook, so each member of the group should have one. The Workbook contains suggestions for worship at the end of each session. Worship is encouraged each time the group meets because it is within worship that caregivers focus on the Source of all caring, hope, and wholeness. It is when caregivers experience that Source that they are enabled to care for others.

A Reading Resource is printed at the end of each session. At times the leader will suggest this resource be used during the session. At other times participants will be encouraged to read the material *following* the session for purposes of review and further insights.

Teaching Methods

The leader will utilize a variety of teaching methods during the training sessions. Most of the methods assume that participants bring a wealth of experience, feelings, and insights that can and should be used to teach one another. There are times when it will be appropriate for the leader to lecture.

One teaching method that is used a great deal is role play. It is quite possible that some participants are uncomfortable with role play. The leader will not ask persons to do something they do not want to do. But role play is a good way to practice skills. In role play one does not pretend something is real, but rather, "acts out" a role. Remember that nearly everyone is in a similar situation in terms of skills. Persons should not worry about how they are doing, since they can even learn from those times when things do not go well.

A Concluding Word

Hopefully, the training experience will be one where participants not only learn and develop caregiving skills, but where persons become caregivers for one another. An important self-understanding on the part of participants is that even the strongest of persons experience hurt. Caregiving is not a matter of the strong helping the weak or of being givers and receivers. Caregiving is a matter of responding to the specific circumstances any one of us might find ourselves in at a given time.

Be prepared for a rich experience in which each participant gives, receives, and hopefully grows toward wholeness.

THEOLOGICAL FOUNDATIONS FOR CARING

Introduction

The Focus of Caring is People

The source of all caring is God's love. It is not God's will that persons should feel alone and trapped in their hurt. It is God's will that in the midst of pain and struggle persons will have hope for a better future and will discover resources in their faith that will enable them to learn and to grow from their experiences. Persons, who themselves have experienced God's care in the midst of pain, become channels through which God's love and care touch the lives of other people.

Purposes of This Session

The purposes of this session are to:
- encourage participants to become better acquainted with each other,
- recall God's caring nature,
- reflect on God's call for all Christians to care, and
- identify some of the participants' gifts for caring.

God is a Caring God

Belief in God as a caring God is deeply rooted in the Bible. What are important stories or events from the Bible that convince you that God is a caring God? Make a list below.

God's Call to Care

God calls Christens to care. To help you think about some of the theological foundations for caring, view the image that will either be shown on an overhead transparency or that is found on the next page.

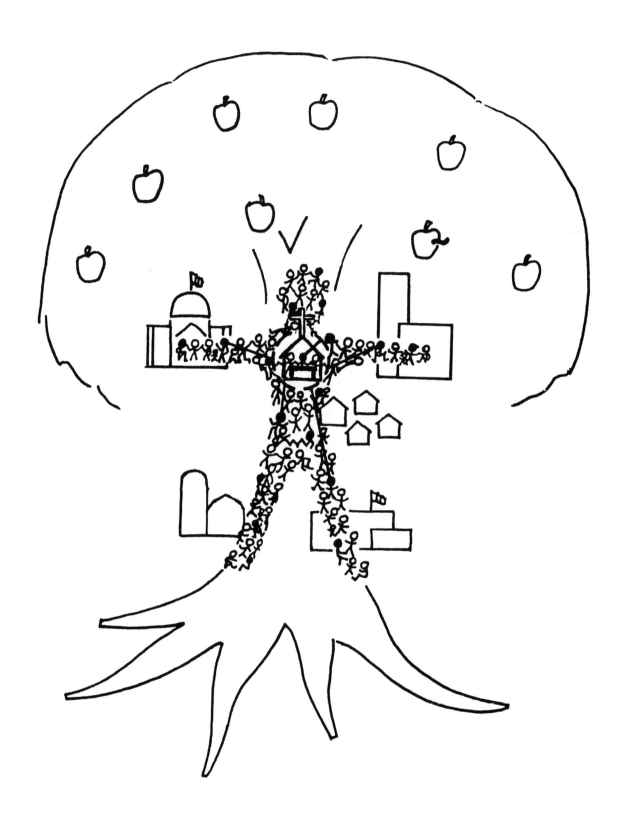

1. Individually, make a note of what you see as you view the image. (No interpretations yet!)

2. As a total group share the interpretations you bring to this image from your understanding and experience of faith. Use this space for your notes. You might want to record some of the insights of others as well.

3. You are encouraged to use the Reading Resource at home to review and gain additional insights on the theological foundations for caring.

God's Gifts for Caring

In calling persons to a ministry of caring, God gives gifts for caring. It is easy for Christians to fall into a "modesty theology" that says one cannot do much in God's reign. It is easy to hold back when one thinks about the assumed task of being a caregiver to those who hurt. One might wonder, "Can I do anything to help?" The answer is that God has given the gifts that are needed for caring.

1. Recall a time when you cared for another person (a family member, neighbor, coworkers, or friend). In silence, briefly give a written description of the situation.

2. What gifts do you think that you used in your caring? Individually, list as many as possible.

3. You might want to note some of the caring gifts others mention as well.

Purpose of a Ministry of Caring

What is the purpose of caring? What is it we hope will happen in the lives of hurting people? You might want to write some of your thoughts below.

Closing Worship

For closing worship, read Galatians 6:2 and I Peter 4:10-11. In a time of prayer the group might thank God for the caring that has been given in their times of hurt, for one another, and for gifts given for caring, and also seek support in their ministry of caring.

A READING RESOURCE

THEOLOGICAL FOUNDATIONS FOR CARING

Introduction

Caring by Christians grows out of an understanding of the nature of God. Caring is empowered by the experience of receiving God's love and care. Those who have experienced hope in the midst of pain, and who were able to grow toward wholeness in the midst of hurt, are called to be caregivers.

God's Caring

Belief in God as a God of care is deeply rooted in the Bible. God's love and care is seen in creation where the universe and persons are brought into being, given resources for survival, and nurtured. God's love and care are seen in expressions of the covenant where freedom replaces slavery and where grace heals broken relationships. The psalmist witnessed to his caring God when he wrote, "The Lord is my shepherd, I shall not want." (Psalm 23:1). The prophet Isaiah pointed to a caring God by saying to a whole nation that was suffering in exile, "Fear not, for I have redeemed you: I have called you by name, you are mine." (Isaiah 43:1).

God's Caring Made Visible in Jesus

God's love and care became evident most clearly in Jesus. Jesus pointed to the caring nature of God in his teachings when he told the parables of the lost (Luke 15), gave the command to do good even to enemies (Luke 6:27-36), and said that it is not the well who need a doctor, but the sick (Matthew 9:9-13).

Jesus pointed to the caring nature of God through his actions when he healed the leper (Mark 1:40-45), the paralytic (Mark 2:3-12), and the centurion's son (Matthew 8:5-10), as well as on the cross where "he died for all...." (2 Corinthians. 5:15).

God's Caring Made Visible Through the Body of Christ

God's love and care continue to be expressed through the Body of Christ (1 Corinthians 12:12-31). All who name the name of Christ, ordained and unordained, have been entrusted with Jesus' ministry of caring. Caring is an expression of the ministry of all Christians. Caring is a fulfillment of the "priesthood of all believers." Caring is a means of God's grace to hurting persons.

Further, God is the one who initiates all caring. Rarely does anyone care as God intends unless that person has first experienced God's care. "We love because God first loved us." (1 John 4:9).

Caring, then, is not so much something good Christians should do. Rather, caring for people who hurt and have experienced loss is a natural response to God's gracious caring.

> But you are a chosen race, a royal priesthood, a holy nation, God's own people, in order that you may proclaim the mighty acts of him who called you out of darkness into his marvelous light. Once you were not a people, but now you are God's people; once you had not received mercy, but now you have received mercy. (1 Peter 2:9-10).

God Gives the Gifts for Caring

The Body of Christ is able to fulfill a ministry of caring because God has given the necessary gifts to members of the Body. God is the source of skills, abilities, and talents that are necessary for caring. Members of the Body of Christ are called to discover, affirm, and develop those gifts for a caring ministry. Some persons seem to have natural gifts for caring. Others develop their gifts through affirmation, training, and experience.

Some of the gifts that God gives for caring are nurturing abilities:
- ✓ availability to persons who hurt,
- ✓ attentive listening,
- ✓ empathy,
- ✓ acceptance,
- ✓ honesty,
- ✓ patience,
- ✓ ability to keep confidences,
- ✓ ability to learn from one's own experiences of hurt,
- ✓ skill in helping persons make connections between their faith and their hurt and loss.

There is a distinction to be made between being a caring person and a professional counselor. A caring person is one human being reaching out to another as they journey together through life. A caring person will use some of the skills and insights gained from professional counselors. You will recognize some of these as you experience this skill training course.

Some of the gifts that God gives are what I call "hands-on skills." These include such things as:
- ✓ running errands,
- ✓ housekeeping or yard work,
- ✓ preparing and providing food.

At times, persons who have those gifts do not always recognize they have them. It then becomes the responsibility of other members of the Body of Christ to challenge the potential in persons, inspire them, support them, and provide training in order that their gifts might blossom, grow, and be used to bring wholeness where there is brokenness.

We have all been gifted to make a difference. The following words from First Peter tell us, "Like good stewards of the manifold grace of God, serve one another with whatever gift each of you has received. Whoever speaks must do so as one speaking the very words of God; whoever serves must do so with the strength that God supplies.... (1 Peter 4:10-11a).

The Purpose of Caring

Those who would be caregivers will be careful not to view hurting persons as being sick or troubled while they see themselves as strong and healthy. The most effective caregivers are those who are in touch with their own pain, who have learned from their experiences, and who have grown toward wholeness. Persons to whom caregivers minister are simply those who are experiencing a significant hurt or loss on their life's journey. The purpose of caring is to relate to these persons in such a way that they too may experience a glimmer of hope and be enabled to grow toward wholeness.

The Arena for Caring

The ministry of caring is a way of being faithful among people who have experienced pain or loss. Caring is not a program to be accomplished at the church. Every day brings the opportunity to care for a family member who has experienced disappointment, a person who moved in next door and is lonely, one who is in pain in a hospital room, a co-worker who has experienced divorce, a friend who has had to retire, or a person at the church whose loved one has died. All of the arenas of day-to-day life provide opportunities to care. One of the reasons that it is critical for the unordained to respond to God's call to care is that they are in every corner of society at any given moment and are able to respond to the hurting persons they see.

Support for Caring

It is not easy to be with people who hurt and have experienced loss. It takes time and energy. There is the responsibility of caregivers to take care of their own needs too. Indeed, there may be times when one does not feel able to reach out and care for others. When one feels dull and barren inside, she or he is not able to give much in relationships; but when one's inner life has been nurtured, one is able to give more.

Those who reach out to touch hurting persons will need to be in touch with the God who loves and cares. Persons in a ministry of caring will not rely on "psyching themselves up" each day, but will seek the resources of faith. Sometimes caring persons will find renewal and direction through their own personal disciplines of Bible study, prayer, and meditation. At other times, they will find support among other caregivers who intentionally gather to share, study, and worship together.

Conclusion

God loves and cares for all persons, especially those who are experiencing pain in their life's journeys. God calls persons to fulfill a ministry of caring as the Body of Christ, gives gifts that are necessary for caring, and provides day-to-day support through the Holy Spirit.

All who name the name of Christ are called to care in their homes, at their work, in the congregation, in their schools, and in the community in order that people who are currently experiencing pain might have hope and be enabled to grow toward wholeness of mind, body, and spirit.

LISTENING AS CARING

Introduction

Being totally present with another person was an important characteristic of Jesus. It is reported that He had compassion for people. One meaning of compassion, "to suffer with," is a basic ingredient to good listening.

Listening is a basic skill that is needed and used in any situation where a person is hurting or has suffered a significant loss. Good listening is a way of being present with another. The focus is on the speaker's concerns. In good listening, one listens for information — that is, what has happened to the person. The listener also listens for meaning. What is the significance of what has happened? What are the feelings about what has happened? The tone of voice is an important key to recognizing the feeling behind the words.

We listen with our eyes, too. Those who study communication suggest that up to 70 percent of communication is nonverbal. If that is so, a good listener will learn to "read" what the body is saying.

Listening that pays attention to words, and the feeling behind the words, is one of the best possible ways to "bear the burdens of one another." Listening does not argue, persuade, or try to fix it right away.

Purposes of the Session

The purposes of this session are to:
- explore some basic principles of good listening,
- identify some of the values of listening, and
- further develop the participants' listening skills through practice.

A Listening Exercise

Four situations where persons experience hurt and loss are printed below. Several possible responses are listed. Check what you believe would be the most helpful response to each person. Better yet, write a response in your own words. The goal of the initial response to a person is to let him or her know that you have heard what has been said and what is being felt. If the leader reads each statement, you will be able to listen to the tone of voice and watch for nonverbal communication.

1. "We just moved to _____. We haven't met many people yet. We miss our close friends. You're the first person to call from your church. The pastor hasn't stopped by yet."

    ____ a.   "I will call the pastor right away and ask that a call be made."

    ____ b.   "It is a lonely time, isn't it?."

    ____ c.   "I found that I had to make the first step in meeting new people."

    ____ d.   "Say more about that."

    ____ e.   "I brought some sweet rolls. Let's make some coffee and talk."

    ____ f.

2. "Having the heart attack has really thrown me for a loop. I don't know if I'm even going to get out of the hospital."

    ____ a.   "You shouldn't say that. Of course, you're going to get better. Just don't think about it, and get plenty of rest."

    ____ b.   "What makes you say that?"

    ____ c.   "I had a heart attack and I'm still going strong."

    ____ d.   "The future doesn't seem too bright right now, does it?"

    ____ e.   "Things will get better."

    ____ f.

3. "There's nothing for me to live for any more. My wife's dead. My kids don't need me. I'm too old to get a job. I don't like to live in this retirement home. I'm just the fifth wheel on a wagon."

    ____ a.   "How long have you felt this way?"

    ____ b.   "You've got a lot to live for. You can love your grandchildren. There are lots of hobbies you can do. You can be active in your church."

    ____ c.   "Let's talk about it."

    ____ d.   "You have certainly had a lot of losses."

_____ e.   "It sounds as if you wonder if life has anything left for you."

_____ f.

4. "I wanted to stop by to have a cup of coffee with you. All the kids are gone now that our son John left town to go to his new job."

_____ a.   "Have you decided what to do with your extra time yet?"

_____ b.   "The house seems kind of empty, huh?"

_____ c.   "You and Joe will have all your time for yourselves now."

_____ d.   "Why don't you get more involved in the church?"

_____ e.   "How does it feel now?"

_____ f.

Evaluation of Responses

Evaluation of the responses will be done in the total group under the direction of the leader. If this resource is being used in a small group of two or three people, turn to the Reading Resource and follow through the material together. You may have some anxiety about whether you have said the right thing or not. It is important to remember that there can be a variety of responses to persons who hurt. Some will be more helpful than others, but it is difficult to talk about right and wrong responses. Furthermore, it will be a unique person who will make the most helpful responses all of the time. The goal of caregivers is to gain new insights and to practice listening skills so that more of our responses to persons with hurt and loss will be helpful.

Review the Reading Resource, _Listening As Caring_, when you have time at home.

Closing Worship

Read Proverbs 20:12 and John 13:34-35.

In a time of prayer, you may want to thank God for being present to each of you. You may feel the need to ask forgiveness for those times when you failed to understand what others around you were feeling. Seek God's guidance in being a better listener. You might close with the words of the following prayer which are usually attributed to St. Francis of Assisi:

"O Divine Master, grant that I
may not so much seek
to be consoled...as to console,
to be understood...as to understand,
to be loved...as to love."

A READING RESOURCE

LISTENING AS CARING

Introduction

Listening is a basic skill needed for caring since listening keeps one's attention on the needs of the person who is hurting or has experienced loss. Caring for others without knowing their needs, we could well be ministering to our own needs, which we project on them.

In addition, a good listener does not try to control or judge. A good listener does not need to agree or disagree. A good listener is open and receptive in trying to understand the other person. The primary focus is on the other's informative statements and feelings.

Evaluating Typical Responses

First, it is important to note at least four stages of using skills in listening:
1. unconscious-unskilled
2. conscious-unskilled
3. conscious-skilled
4. unconscious-skilled

Some of these listening skills may feel uncomfortable for you now; those feelings remind you that you are passing through the stages. Keep using the listening skills until you feel more natural with them.

There are some responses in the listening exercise that will normally be more helpful than others. Some of the responses even run the risk of blocking further sharing between persons. The relationships you have to the other persons makes a difference in the blocking effect. You will note that the less helpful responses tend to focus only on the words the person expressed.

A. Sometimes our responses to hurting persons suggest that we do not believe they are capable of solving their own problem. When we give quick and easy answers we often miss the real feeling that was behind the words. As a result the person may resist us. Worse yet, our solution could be wrong for them.

    1a. "I will call the pastor right away and ask her to stop by."

    4d. "Why don't you get more involved in the church?"

B. Other responses reflect our need to get information rather than our need to identify with what the person might be feeling. It is helpful to ask ourselves how we would use the information.

    3a. "How long have you felt this way?"

    4a. "Have you decided how to use your extra time yet?"

    2e. "Things will get better." (They may not.)

C. At other times, our words are meant to offer reassurance. That is a natural thing for caring persons to do. But if reassurance is given too quickly, it may not be heard. Strong negative feelings may block hearing what could be altogether appropriate at a later time in the conversation. At other times, the person may not continue talking because he or she senses that we do not understand what is being felt, or that we do not think those feelings are very important.

2c. "I had a heart attack and I'm still going strong."

4c. "You and Joe will have all your time for yourselves now."

D. Sometimes our responses indicate that we believe we can help another person deal with their hurt or loss through the use of logic. Logic tends to focus on words and not feelings. The result is that the person might well argue with us over the logic that has been used.

1c. "I found that I had to make the first step in meeting new people."

3b. "You've got a lot to live for. You can love your grandchildren. There are lots of hobbies you can do. You can be active in your church."

E. At other times, our responses indicate that we want to avoid recognizing the person's feelings. When we do that, the implication is made that one should avoid life's difficult moments rather than deal with them in a faithful manner.

2a. "You shouldn't say that."

F. Other responses do not identify what the person is feeling, but they do not carry the danger of stopping communication either. In a sense, the words are an invitation to say more.

1d. "Say more about that."

2b. "What makes you say that?"

3c. "Let's talk about it."

4e. "How does it feel now?"

G. Sometimes our responses get behind the words to get in touch with what a person is feeling. When that happens there is a sense of being with the person who is hurting.

1b. "It's a lonely time, isn't it?"

2d. "The future doesn't look too bright right now, does it?"

3d. "You certainly have had a lot of losses."

4b. "The house seems kind of empty, huh?"

H. There are times when silence, a noncommittal response such as, "I see," a touch, or a hug might be ways of being with a person and of encouraging him or her to continue to share with you. Be sensitive to whether or not the person is comfortable with a touch or hug.

Some Values of Good Listening

Persons who have been especially helpful to another will often say, "But all I did was listen." Think about what good listening can do.

- Good listening keeps the listener from giving quick advice or instant solutions that might not fit a person's needs. Rather, you help the hurting person identify and implement his or her own solutions. Listening assumes that each of us has truth within. The Christ in us is a source of guidance deep within our souls.

- When a person feels he or she has really been heard, a sense of warmth is created. One person said, "I felt cared for."

- Persons who are listened to indicate a spirit of trust begins to develop

18

between them and the listener. When trust develops, deeper hurts and needs are shared. Morton T. Kelsey puts it beautifully in *Caring* when he says that we only let others come close to us when they "knock with listening care."

- Good listening encourages the other person to talk. Good listening helps them name the pain they are feeling. Talking itself tends to reduce strong feelings so that a person can focus energy on dealing with the problem at hand. At other times, talking enables a person to put "jumbled ideas and feelings" into some order where new insights and possible solutions become clearer.

- The experience of being listened to encourages hope. The listener might even be the avenue through which God's presence is experienced. Remember, ours is an incarnational faith. *spiritual*

- Finally, good listening may make it possible for our speaking to be heard. When careful listening takes place, persons are more likely to hear and value what the listener says.

Conclusion

The goal in listening is the same as it is in loving — to feel acceptance, to be enabled to grow and to be encouraged to take responsibility for one's own life.

In good listening we offer ourselves to others so that the living Christ can be present to them. Indeed, we are the Body of Christ among persons who hurt and have experienced loss.

Session 3

SPEAKING IN CARING WAYS

Introduction

Listening is a key that opens the door to a caring relationship, but there is a time for speaking as well. There is a time to share information, insights, and provide guidance. Indeed, one who listens carefully will be heard when the moment comes to speak. Speaking in caring ways is a skill that can be developed just as in the case of good listening. Speaking is a basic skill for caring. There are insights to share out of one's experience. There is a story to tell that grows out of one's faith journey. There are opportunities to put people in touch with powerful belief systems. The real issue is how one can speak in ways that bring healing, hope, and growth.

Purposes of the Session

The purposes of this session are to:
- introduce participants to some guidelines for speaking in caring ways,
- demonstrate helpful ways of sharing one's own experience,
- reflect on the use of the Bible and prayer in caring, and
- further develop speaking skills through practice.

A Speaking Exercise

Following are four situations where persons experience hurt and loss. Several possible responses are listed. Check what you believe would be the most helpful thing to say to each person. Better yet, write your own response. For purposes of this exercise, assume that you have been visiting for several moments and that you have already used some of your best listening skills. You are now ready to explore dimensions of hope and possible choices to help deal with the hurt and loss that has been experienced.

Follow the directions of the leader if you are in a larger group. If this material is being used in a small group of two or three people, read each situation together. As a group decide what would be the most appropriate response to each person.

1. You have been visiting with Linda about her being out of work and her inability to find another job, when she says, "Worst of all, my unemployment benefits are about to run out. I just don't know what I'm going to do. I've even thought about dropping out of church because I can't keep up my pledge."

_____ a. "Don't do that. We need you at the church. Your are good at so many things."

_____ b. "Remember what the Bible says about trusting God for what tomorrow might bring."

_____ c. "Try praying about it."

_____ d. "I sense your struggle. Is there any ray of hope? Is there anything in your faith experience to help?"

_____ e.

2. You are visiting with a friend who has had a divorce. In the conversation, he has expressed anger, confusion, and a sense of guilt. He says, "One of the things I struggle with most is loneliness. I just don't like being alone."

_____ a. "I know just how you feel. I went through exactly the same thing."

_____ b. "One of the things I struggled with in my loneliness was to use that time as an opportunity to feel more positive about my being single again. It was a chance to work at feeling good about myself. Have you thought much about that possibility for yourself?"

_____ c. "The Bible tells us that we are never alone in that God is always with us."

_____ d. "Are you aware of the new support group for divorced persons at the church?

_____ e.

3. You are aware of the Smiths' problem with alcoholism. Mrs. Smith has talked about the stress her husband's drinking has caused. One day she stops by and says, "I can't take it any more. I'm going to leave."

_____ a. "Can you do that when the Bible has such strong statements against divorce?"

_____ b. "Have you talked to the pastor about your problem? He has had some special training in working with alcoholism in families."

_____ c. "Oh, you can make it okay. God never gives us more than we can handle."

_____ d. "I will be praying for you."

_____ e.

4. The wife of your close friend died a year ago. You have visited together and cried together many times. On this particular visit he says, "I don't understand why I can't get back to normal. I pray for that, but I don't feel God hears."

_____ a.   "I know something about that experience. I felt much the same way after my spouse died. I discovered that getting 'back to normal' takes more time for some than for others. It was nearly a year before my times of grief grew less severe."

_____ b.   "Your feelings are real, but not unusual. Even great religious leaders have wondered about God's presence in time of need. The psalmist once cried out, 'My God, my God! Why have you forsaken me?' "

_____ c.   "Keep praying. God answers all prayer."

_____ d.   "Have you decided when you are going to visit your daughter yet?"

_____ e.

Evaluation of Responses

Evaluation of the responses will be done in the total group under the direction of the leader. If this resource is being used in a small group of two or three people, turn to the Reading Resource and follow through material together.

As with listening, you may have some anxiety about whether you are saying the right thing or not. There are a variety of responses we might make to people who hurt or have experienced loss. Some of our words will be equally helpful. The goal of this session is to gain some insight into the effect of some of our responses to persons toward the end that what we say will be more helpful and hopeful.

Review the Reading Resource, *Speaking in Caring Ways*, when you have time at home.

Suggestions for an Expanded Session

Suggestion A:
CAREFRONTING
(Confrontation in a Caring Way)

Confrontation is a caring act! The Bible says, "Speaking the truth in love, we are to grow up in every way into Him who is the Head, into Christ (Ephesians 4:14 RSV).

Carefronting is important when persons:
- ✓ do not want to take action needed at a time of hurt,
- ✓ are involved in self-destructive behavior,
- ✓ disrupt family or group life,
- ✓ take advantage of your caring spirit.

When you confront in a caring way, there are several key steps to keep in mind:

1. Confront persons in private, not in front of others.

2. Describe in non-blaming or non-judgmental language what the person is doing or saying.

3. After confronting, use your best listening skills. The person may share important insights with you.

4. Keep the unacceptable behavior before the person. The behavior must not be allowed to continue.

5. Ask the person what he or she intends to do about the behavior that has been confronted. You may make some suggestions, but let the person decide on the final course of action.

Carefronting is risky. Relationships may be strained or broken. However, confrontation in a caring way can result in personal growth and more effective discipleship.

Suggestion B:
INTERCESSORY PRAYER AS CARING

Praying for others opens our lives both to God and to the one for whom we pray. Through intercessory prayer we invite God to minister through us.

Recall a time when you knew someone else was praying for you. If you do not know of such a time, remember a time when you prayed for someone else. You might want to close your eyes as you think of the situation. Make a mental note of some of the feelings you had. Reflect on what it meant to you.

24

Share your experience with one other person in the group.

Closing Worship

Bring to mind the name of a person about whom you are especially concerned today. In silence, pray for her or him. Does God seem to be urging you to reach out to that person in some way — a visit, a note, or practical help? If so, make a decision to follow that urging.

Read 2 Corinthians 2:14-17 (RSV). Especially note the images of "peddlers of the word" and "the aroma of Christ."

Conclude with a brief spoken prayer together.

A READING RESOURCE

SPEAKING IN CARING WAYS

Introduction

Speaking in caring ways is a basic skill for the caregiver. Speaking is a way to share something of yourself with other persons so they might sense that their hurt and loss is not so unusual and they are not alone. Speaking is a way to share insights from one's faith experience, and to give a glimmer of hope to those who are struggling in their journey.

The question is, "How can one speak so as to encourage healing and growth?"

Evaluating Speaking Responses

There are some responses in the speaking exercise that will normally be more helpful than others.

A. Speaking will generally be more helpful if we respond to the actual needs the person has expressed. What the person says should trigger our words. Most of the statements in the previous exercise do that, though some of those responses have less helpful characteristics. Changing the subject is one of the things listeners often do so they themselves will feel more comfortable.

   1a. "Don't do that. We need you at the church."

   4d. "Have you decided when you are going to visit your daughter yet?"

It is important to remember that hurting persons are usually more willing to talk about their experiences and how they feel about them than we are to hear them.

B. Pat answers and clichés are usually not helpful responses. When we are not always sure what to say, it is easy to slip into what seem to be eternal truths. It is an attempt to keep the world orderly and understandable. Pat answers and clichés tend to apply to everyone, but hurt and pain is so personal. The fact is that these truths are not usually experienced as being helpful because they are not personal enough.

   1b. "Remember what the Bible says about trusting God for what tomorrow might bring."

   2c. "The Bible tells us that we are never alone in that God is always with us."

   3c. "Oh, you can make it okay. God never gives us more than we can handle."

   4c. "Keep praying. God answers all prayer."

   Keep in mind the experience of people. Some persons may be responsive to Bible verses and prayer because that is their devotional approach to all of life.

C. While sharing the insights of faith may be appropriate, it is usually not helpful to tell hurting persons what we think they should believe or what good Christians should do.

   1c. "Try praying about it."

3a. "Can you do that when the Bible has such strong statements against divorce?"

When we share faith perspectives, it is usually more helpful to speak out of our own understanding of faith and out of our own experience.

4b. "Your feelings are real, but not unusual. Even great religious leaders have wondered about God's presence in the time of need."

At other times it may be helpful to ask questions that encourage the one who is hurting to think about the resources of faith. Belief systems can be freeing and healing.

1d. "I sense your struggle. Is there any ray of hope? Is there anything in your faith experience to help?"

A danger in sharing our own faith experiences is that we go into too much detail. As speakers, we can easily monopolize the conversation. When we do that, the attention has turned from the hurting person to the caregiver.

D. It is often helpful to share some of our own experiences. The caregiver will always avoid saying, "I know just how you feel" (2a). However, there are times when one might say he or she has had similar experiences or feelings. To say to a hurting person that we can identify with them, helps build a bridge for further caring. When we share something of ourselves it may help the other person feel understood. The sharing of our own struggles, doubts, and pain also demonstrates that caregiving is not a matter of the strong helping the weak. Rather, it is a reminder that hurt and loss touch all of us at some time during our lives. It will be important to remember that sharing something of ourselves helps make a connection with the other person. It is not a time for the caregiver to unburden himself or herself.

2b. "One of the things I struggled with in my loneliness...."

4a. "I know something of that experience."

E. Sometimes the most caring thing we can do is to encourage a person to seek the help of a professionally trained person. There are usually some clear warning signals that indicate when a trained person might be helpful:

✓ Significant change in sleeping and eating patterns.
✓ Inability to concentrate at work.
✓ Increasing tensions with family, friends, and co-workers.

There are several steps to take if the warning signals are clear:

✓ Tell the person of the warning signals you have noticed. Describe them.
✓ Suggest there are some things with which a trained professional can help.
✓ Feel free to tell the person what a trained person has meant to you if you have ever turned to one for help.
✓ Be prepared to recommend a person who might be contacted. You might contact the specialist first to see if they have any advice on how to approach the hurting person.

✓ Encourage the hurting person to make the contact. You should not do it. Not everyone will follow through on your recommendation to seek help. Persons need to have the freedom to choose. No matter what happens, continue to keep up your caring contact.

F. Sometimes the Bible can be used in caring ways. The Bible is a source of strength, hope, insight, and inspiration. Biblical references seem to carry more power when they are shared out of memory in direct response to a need that has been expressed. In a sense, one calls on a treasury of inspiration to illustrate, to clarify, and to provide a dimension of hope.

4b. "The psalmist once cried out, 'My God, my God! Why have you forsaken me?' "

G. Finally, prayer is important to caring people. First of all, prayer puts caregivers in touch with the source of power and with the center of the hurting person. It is appropriate to pray with people who are in the midst of struggle. Spoken prayer between persons should deal honestly with the feelings and hurt that have been expressed. Second, it is always appropriate to pray for hurting persons in our personal devotional lives.

3d. "I will be praying for you." Intercessory prayer brings the deepest needs of persons into the sphere where the healing work of Christ can take place.

Conclusion

To speak in caring ways is to speak in response to the hurting person's needs. In some instances, that may simply mean we give specific answers to a request for information. It is important to remember that no one can change history. The comment, "You should have...," is not helpful. At another time, it may mean sharing the insights that have come to us in similar life-shaping events. To speak in caring ways is to help another person problem solve. Work with them to identify the real issues, look at a variety of options for decisions, and then encourage them to decide and move on to another place. It might be that we are with another person at just the right time to help that person make the important connection between his or her story and God's story.

OPPORTUNITIES FOR CARING CONTACTS

Introduction

There are many opportunities to make caring contacts, because there is so much hurt in the lives of people around us. Some of that hurt is quite visible. When a major crisis such as serious illness, accident, divorce, or death occurs, we are aware of the need to reach out with care. We may not always be as sensitive to some of the expected crises that come as a normal part of life. When one changes jobs, moves to a new community, retires, or one's children leave home, we may not be mindful of the significant stress that is experienced. What is needed are lay persons who are trained to recognize and respond to hurts, especially those hurts that are not as easily detected as others.

Availability is a basic caregiving gift. While being available is a characteristic of a caring person, it can be developed much like a skill.

Purposes of the Session

The purposes of this session are to:
- become more sensitive to the variety of opportunities to care,
- examine some helpful steps in making a caring contact, and
- practice making a caring contact.

Opportunities for Caring

There are many opportunities for caring, because there are so many persons who experience a variety of hurts. Some of those hurts occur as people move through the stages of their lives:
- ✓ leaving home and friends to begin a new job,
- ✓ children leaving home,
- ✓ retirement.

Some of the hurt persons experience is more crisis-oriented:
- ✓ serious illness,
- ✓ loss of a job,
- ✓ divorce,
- ✓ death of a spouse, child, or other loved one.

Develop two kinds of lists:

1. Think of your congregation, neighborhood, and community. What are some of the hurts that come immediately to mind?

2. Reflect on your own life. List as many hurts as you can recall, great and small.

You will be invited to share some hurts from your lists, but only as you feel comfortable doing. All hurts generated by you and your group provide opportunities for caring by you and others.

First, this "Opportunities for Caring" experience reminds us that many small hurts cause stress in the lives of persons. We will be able to identify and take more seriously some of the stress people experience.

Second, people under stress are also open to the possibility of growth and change. People are often in an "unfrozen" stage, a time when they are both open to care-receiving, and to change. Persons tend to deal with stress in more effective ways if they have significant relationships to caring persons. The good news of forgiveness and acceptance shared by a caring person in word or modeled can be an important resource in dealing with some of the stress-producing events people experience.

Finally, the "Opportunities for Caring" experience can help us become aware of our own need for support and caring as we make our life journey.

Making a Caring Contact

Follow along in the Reading Resource as the leader highlights some important steps to consider once you decide to visit someone under stress or who has had a significant loss.

If you are using this material in a group of two or three persons, simply read and discuss the material together.

A Caring Contact Role Play

This will be the first role play that you will experience in these training sessions. The leader will give clear instructions and guidelines. You may want to read the notes on role play in the Introduction to your Workbook. If you have never done a role play before, you are encouraged to try it. The possibilities for learning are significant.

In the space below, you may want to write a few notes from the discussion you will have after the role play.

Closing Worship

Read James 5:13-16 or Luke 8:40-54. Both references reflect the caring gift of availability.

In silence, think of someone who might be under stress from some less obvious pain, loss, or life experience. Pray for her or him. Plan to visit the person.

Close with prayer together. If you have not already done so, you might reach out and touch one another in your group.

A READING RESOURCE

MAKING A CARING CONTACT

There are several different types of visits one might make to people. There is the friendly visit where the visitors want to become acquainted and desire to tell about the church and its program. There is the evangelistic visit which tends to emphasize the verbal witness to one's faith. There is a caring visit which is usually made in response to some perceived need. While all types of visits have their time and place, the caring visit is the focus of this Resource.

Availability is a basic characteristic of a person who would make a caring visit. One becomes available by going to persons who hurt and by responding to those who have some of the less obvious pain. One becomes available by being totally present to the person being visited. The caregiver has no other agenda than that of the needs of the person visited. One becomes available by making additional visits or by responding with practical action if that is needed. While availability is a characteristic or a gift that has been given to the caregiver, there is also a sense in which it is a skill to be developed.

The caring visit is most effective when it is done by one person. Some visitation guidelines suggest that persons go in teams, but visiting a person under stress seems more natural and real when it is done by one person. It is easier for one person to keep the conversation focused. It is easier to share in a more open and honest way with one person. It is easier to develop a sense of trust with one person.

In preparing for a caring visit there are several practical steps to consider. First of all, you need to decide about making a telephone call. Whether or not you call depends on the nature of the community. Do people normally call before they visit, or do they just drop in? Whether or not you call may depend on the nature of your relationship. If you do not know a person well and you plan to visit because of an organized program, you may want to call ahead. If the person you plan to visit is a friend, you may simply want to stop by. Second, be clear about the reason for your visit. Have you become aware of significant stress or a crisis in the life of the one to be visited? Third, be aware of your own feelings. It is natural to feel some anxiety about making contact with someone who is experiencing a significant hurt. Fourth, consider prayer before you visit to help you deal with your own feelings and to help you be open to God's Spirit that will work through you. Fifth, decide what to say ahead of time for only the first part of your visit. If you are visiting someone you do not know, such a new person in your neighborhood, you will want to say who you are, why you are at their home, and ask if it is convenient to visit. If it is someone you know, simply be open and to the point about your visit. You might say that you have just become aware of a certain event or series of events in that person's life, and you were wondering how the person was getting along.

Then play it by ear. Use your best listening skills to determine the person's thoughts and feelings. Be prepared to spend some time if you sense there is a need to talk, for companionship, or to make some difficult decision. Your caring presence may be the most important thing you can give. Many of life's stressful events leave persons with a deep sense of loneliness.

In your visit, there may be the opportunity to share your faith, to explore a ray of hope, and to pray together. Let the speaking opportunities grow naturally out of your conversation together.

Do not feel you have to stay for a long time. You can usually sense when it is time to depart. Simply express appreciation for your time together. You may become aware of a specific task you can volunteer to do. Promise to return only if that is possible for you.

There will be times, indeed many times, when the visit with a hurting person will not be in the home. The caring contact may take place during a coffee break, on the mall of a shopping center, or in the corner of the church after a meeting. You may open up a significant 15-20 minute conversation by simply saying that you are aware of a hurt or loss and you are wondering how things are going.

If certain events cause stress in our lives, we can be sure that those same events will cause stress in the lives of others as well. Hurting persons often wonder why people, even friends, do not talk about the loss and the pain in their lives. The caring person will take the initiative to reach out. Availability is a caring gift.

CARING FOR PERSONS WHO EXPERIENCE DIVORCE

Introduction

Divorce is a fact of our life together. Indeed, there is a rise in divorce statistics. It is experienced by adults of every age.

Our task in this Session is not to attack divorce or to defend it, but to discover ways to care for those who experience it.

Purposes of the Session

The purposes of this session are to:
- increase the participants' awareness of their own attitudes toward persons who have experienced divorce,
- identify some of the feelings and experiences of those who have been divorced, and
- practice making a visit using any new insights that have been gained.

Attitudes Toward Divorce

One of the caring responses we might make to persons who are divorced is to explore some of our own attitudes toward that experience. In the space below, list some of the thoughts and feelings you have when you hear of the divorce of a close acquaintance.

Describe how you normally react to a person who has been divorced. What do you say or do, and not say or do?

These are personal reflections and will not be shared with anyone. You will be asked to review them at the end of the session.

The Experience of Divorce

We can be more caring to persons who hurt if we have an idea of what their experience is like. As thoughts and feelings are generated by the group you may want to take some notes.

Caring Responses to Persons Who Experience Divorce

Once we have an idea of what a person's hurt and loss is like, we are able to make more caring responses. As ideas are generated by the group, you might want to make a list of the helpful things we can do and say to persons who experience divorce.

It is sometimes good to be aware of the things we do or say that are not helpful. As the group develops some of these responses you may want to make a note of them.

Review the Reading Resource at home for additional insights.

Visiting a Person Who is Divorced — A Role Play

Role play is learning through experience. It gives participants a chance to practice their skills with a minimum of risk. We can even learn from the less-than-helpful things we do and say.

The leader will give details and instruction for the role play. Use the space below for any notes from the discussion after the role play.

Personal Reflection on Attitudes Toward Divorce

Turn back to the notes you made about your own attitudes and actions toward persons who have experienced divorce. As a result of this session, were any of your attitudes and feelings confirmed? What insights did you gain? What changes might you make? Make a note of some of your thoughts. You will not need to share these reflections unless you should choose to do so.

Closing Worship

Read Galatians 6:4-5 (TEV) and Matthew 9:10-13 (TEV).

In prayer, you might affirm the worth of each person, claim the promise of God's forgiveness, celebrate the hope for new beginnings, and make the commitment to hold persons who experience divorce — including children who are involved — in the caring fellowship of the Body of Christ.

A READING RESOURCE

CARING FOR PERSONS WHO EXPERIENCE DIVORCE

Introduction

Divorce is a fact of our life together. It is experienced by adults of every age. Florence Lund Williams and R. Poe Williams, writing in *Ages and Stages*, suggest that young adults consider divorce when they review their earlier commitments in light of their present goals; middle age adults consider divorce when they express their individuality in a marriage that has been built on one partner being subordinate to the other; older adults consider divorce when the major responsibilities of a marriage that has been in name only are fulfilled.[1]

The task of caring persons is not to attack divorce or to apologize for it, but to find ways to be more caring of the people who experience it. What has happened cannot be changed. How persons deal with their divorce can be affected in positive ways by caring people.

The Experience of Divorce and Some Caring Responses

Caregivers will want to be sensitive to the complex feelings and experiences of persons who are divorced and who are divorcing. There is hurt and a sense of loss, but there are also new possibilities for life.

Most persons who experience divorce report grief, just as in the loss of a loved one through death. Indeed, there has been the

---

[1] Williams, Florence Lund and R. Poe Williams. "Divorce." *Ages and Stages.* Nashville: United Methodist Publishing House, 1982, p.45.

loss of a relationship and the loss of one's dream. The intensity of the grief depends upon the length of the marriage, the quality of the relationship, the presence or absence of children, and the financial condition of the persons involved.

The tragedy is that one does not grieve as publicly at the time of divorce as at the time of death. Friends and relatives usually do not travel long distances to be with those who hurt. People do not respond to the "loss" with cards, flowers, memorials, or food. There is no public ritual to help with the expression of grief.

A CARING RESPONSE: If you are friends with one or both persons who have been divorced, be open and honest about the divorce. Do not pretend nothing has happened. Be there! Give the persons time to deal with their grief. Use your best listening skills to avoid pat answers and well-meaning advice. Utilize all forms of contact by visiting in the home, on the street, or after meetings. Write notes, make phone calls, and issue invitations to events that are not just for couples. Loneliness is a real and difficult experience to which friends can respond.

Many persons who experience divorce report feelings of guilt, a dimension of grief. They may wonder if they neglected the relationship, if they should have started the divorce process, or if they are to blame for the divorce. For some, especially those who have been active in church, the guilt often grows out of the strong emphasis the church places on marriage and against divorce.

A CARING RESPONSE: Encourage persons to talk of their guilt. Recognize that it is a real feeling, but not an uncommon one. By word and by acceptance, remind them of God's forgiveness, the chance to learn and grow from the experience, and the hope for a new beginning.

Anger is an emotion reported by many divorced persons. It is another dimension of grief. Anger may emerge out of a sense of being rejected by the other person. There may be a strong desire to get even or to hurt the other. When children are involved, they are often used by one parent against the other. Sometimes the anger is kept inside and leads to depression.

A CARING RESPONSE: Encourage the expression of anger through your best listening skills. Reflect back to the person what you sense he or she feels. Provide for some time of silence to let the person express what is being felt. Later in the conversation, or at a later date, you may suggest a visit with the pastor or a professional counselor if the person is not already doing so.

Some persons who go through a divorce struggle with a sense of self-worth. They may feel unlovable, especially if they were the ones who were left. Lack of self-esteem may express itself in dependency upon others, in self-pity, or in the belief that they will never have a significant relationship again.

A CARING RESPONSE: Continue to affirm persons who experience divorce as persons of worth and dignity. Encourage in them a sense of self-worth by continuing a close relationship with them, by including them in some of the old activities, and by challenging them to pursue new tasks.

An overall caring response might be to encourage participation in a church or community support group for persons who experience divorce. If a support group does not exist, see if you can help start one. A support group provides the arena to share similar experiences and feelings openly and honestly, to deal with practical needs as determined by group members (finances, parenting, entertainment, new relationships, sexuality, housekeeping functions, etc.), to help set goals for the next few months or years, to utilize the best insights of theology and psychology to help participants interpret what is happening and can happen in their lives, and to experience healing and wholeness.

Many persons who experience divorce report a change in the attitude of people around them, including in the church. Some people report finding care and acceptance in their community of faith, from another congregation in their community, or from individual clergy and laity. But many persons speak of turning to the church for help only to experience avoidance, coldness, and embarrassment. There are constant questions and whispered rumors. Members take sides. The loss of the ministry of the church at a time of such hurt usually leads to additional anger. The negative reaction from persons who value marriage highly probably comes for various reasons. Some have strong feelings against divorce (and divorced persons) because of their religious beliefs. Others may sense a threat to their own marriage. They do not lack in caring so much as they feel insecure in their own relationship. Finally, some persons just do not know how to relate to someone who has experienced divorce.

A CARING RESPONSE: One caring response might be to become aware of your own feelings about divorce and divorced persons. Do you find yourself being drawn away from or drawn toward persons whose marriage has ended? You may sense some tension between the teachings of Jesus on divorce and marriage and his teachings on grace. This is not the place for a lengthy reflection on marriage and divorce as seen in the teachings of Jesus, but that is an area you might want to pursue.

As caring persons, we might help our community of faith explore its general attitudes toward divorce and persons who have that experience. Caring persons will teach and model forgiveness and reconciliation. They will model a spirit of understanding and acceptance. Caring persons will help persons express their grief. Caring congregations will provide support groups. Persons have the same talents and usually the same commitments following a divorce as they did before. Be sensitive to how groups plan and talk about ministry to people. There is a tendency to think in terms of "traditional family" images when a church carries out its ministry.

It is easy to forget children in the midst of divorce. The two main persons involved receive most the attention. Small children may feel they will be abandoned. Older children may feel they helped cause the divorce. Sometimes children are used by one parent against the other. At other times children manipulate their divorced parents.

Give special attention to children. The decision to divorce can be overwhelming to them. The decision may come as a total surprise that catches children off guard. They have no choice in the matter. Change is sudden for many children. A sense of security and constancy will be gone.

Children may take partial blame for the divorce of their parents. It is important to say over and over to the children, "You did not cause the divorce. You cannot mend the relationship."

Children often feel rejected by the parent who leaves. Even though there is regular contact, that parent is not around the house all the time as before.

It is also important to remember that it may be difficult for children to trust that someone who loves them won't hurt them again. Trust may be the most important emotion to rebuild.

A CARING RESPONSE: Risk talking to children. Initiate conversation with them. Do not wait for them to initiate talk with you. Be patient with some of their acting-out behavior.

■   Encourage children to have a relationship to an adult, to share feelings, and to ask questions. Provide a listening ear. Give children a chance to talk about the divorce and their feelings about it. Trust will grow.

■   Encourage parents to keep children appraised of the divorce process from the beginning. Encourage them to help children understand the divorce. As caregivers to divorcing parents, encourage them to resist bad-mouthing the other parent in the presence of their children, but rather to be open and honest about problems in the marriage.

■   Provide leadership in the congregation to understand how divorce affects children and how the congregation can be caring; in addition, help to develop support groups for children.

■   Be careful not to speak of inviting "mothers and fathers" to church events for families or of always using traditional images of the family. Speak of "parent or parents."

Persons often re-marry after divorce as one expression of new possibilities. Stepfamilies account for a large percentage of American families. There is even a stepfamily association in the United States. Stepfamilies have their own unique problems. They are often born out of the pain and struggle of divorce, which is sometimes carried over to the next marriage. There are unique issues related to parenting and discipline, patterns of communication, and loyalty to the absent parent.

A CARING RESPONSE: Instant families need special care. Individuals and the congregation can help parents of the step-families be aware of some of the unique problems, help parents identify and discuss with their children any unique feelings they have, and help parents prepare for all the positive possibilities of new relationships and new interests. If you have the opportunity, encourage step-families to develop new traditions and family rituals.

Finally, persons who experience divorce usually see new possibilities for their lives. Divorce is not all tragedy. The growth task needed following a divorce is to establish a sense of one's own identity and separateness where that has not existed before. Following a divorce, one might choose new directions for life. Energy once spent in marital conflict can be used to develop new interests, to set and strive for new goals, and to develop new relationships.

A CARING RESPONSE: Do not try to console a person who has experienced divorce as if something terrible has happened. While there may be a great deal of hurt, many persons believe they have taken a positive step in seeking a divorce. Be a sounding board as they make decisions, set goals, and develop plans.

Conclusion

Whether a person has initiated a divorce or is the one who is divorced, many of the dynamics discussed here are similar. For example, guilt will be present in both persons, but for different reasons. The one divorced will probably have more intense feelings of rejection, but persons who initiate the divorce often describe a similar feeling prior to the divorce action itself.

Hopefully, it is clear that those who experience divorce need sensitive caregivers who do not judge but accept, who do not reject but provide a ray of hope, who do not dwell on failure but encourage growth toward wholeness.

WHEN FRIENDS LOSE THEIR JOB

Introduction

Unemployment and underemployment are harsh realities of our time. While persons have always been out of work in our society, the numbers of unemployed or underemployed persons have increased and have become more visible. Those looking for work include executives, construction and clerical workers. Predictions indicate that unemployment will continue at a high rate because we are in the midst of a change in the job market. Some old jobs will not even be available when the economy recovers, and it will take time for workers to learn new skills.

An important part of this unemployment picture is the attitude of those who are employed. When a community experiences serious unemployment, such as when a major industry closes down or relocates, there seems to be greater support for the unemployed. When the unemployment picture in a community is not so dismal, the attitude toward the unemployed may be quite negative and critical, or not acknowledged.

Purposes of the Session

The purposes of this session are to:
- help participants become more aware of community attitudes toward persons who are unemployed,
- explore some of the thoughts and feelings of persons who are without work,
- examine a variety of caring responses that might be made by individuals or by a congregation, and
- practice making a visit utilizing any new insights gained in this session.

The Reality of Unemployment

If you are asked to move into groups of three to reflect on the attitude of your community toward persons who are unemployed or underemployed, you might want to make notes of your discussion here. List words or images that people in your community use when they talk about those who are without work or who are underemployed. (You may be asked to do this same listing individually.)

43

If an unemployed person shares his or her experience with you, make some notes that you can refer to later.

If a small group of two or three persons is using this material, you will want to read about the experience of being unemployed in the Reading Resource. Some discussion questions to use with the printed material might be:

✓ "Did you gain any new insights?"

✓ "Is there anything in the material with which you disagree?"

✓ "Is there anything you would add?"

Caring Responses to the Unemployed Worker

Now for the important question. In light of the thoughts and feelings of persons who are without work, what kind of caring responses would be expressions of God's love and concern through us?

As ideas are listed by the total group you may want to make some notes for yourself. Some ideas are listed in the Reading Resource, but it is meant to be a suggestive list only.

If persons in your group have had the experience of unemployment or underemployment, you might want to record their reflections on how your caring responses would be experienced by them.

Role Play of a Visit to an Unemployed Worker

The leader will give you instructions for the role play. Use the space below to note any observations or ideas that come from the discussion after the role play.

Closing Worship

Read Luke 1:46-55 and/or Luke 16:19-31. Note the special concern Jesus had for the poor and the powerless.

In a time of prayer, remember specific persons who are unemployed. Pray for them during the week. You might want to include a time of personal dedication as you seek to be a more caring person.

THE UNEMPLOYED/UNDEREMPLOYED WORKER AND CARING

Introduction

Being unemployed (or failing in business or farming) in a society that places such high value on work and productivity, can be a jarring experience. Sustained unemployment and business failure can be a tragedy for individual workers, the family, and the community.

There is something implicit in the Christian faith that urges us to respond to the pain and loss of persons who have been pushed to the margins of society.

The Experience of Being Unemployed

Imagine how it must feel to lose one's productivity and source of financial security in our kind of society. There will be grief because there has been a significant loss. Part of that grief will be expressed in anger — at employers, government policies or themselves. At other times the grief will express itself in guilt — over not providing for one's family or for not pursuing another vocation.

When one loses a job, there is a sense of rejection. The newly unemployed person obviously thinks, "I am no longer needed here." The longer an unsuccessful job search continues, the more the sense of rejection increases. One might follow all of the suggestions on how to seek employment only to discover that none of them works for him or her. One person exclaimed, "I can't stand being turned down again."

After some time, the erosion of self-esteem will probably occur. If work and worth go hand in hand, as it seems to in our society, one without work for a period of time begins to question his or her worth as a person. A common feeling is, "There must be something wrong with me."

There are feelings of failure. There is often embarrassment in seeking assistance from others or in even being around friends who are still working. There is anxiety about whether they will find work or not. One person said, "There is little chance that I will be hired." Another said, "Every time I was asked why I was home, it felt like a knife in the ribs."

A predominant feeling is powerlessness, a feeling that grows as time lapses. In our society, having money is power. Without money how can a person secure what his or her family needs to survive? "How can I pay my bills?" "How can I lessen the hurt my family feels?" In our society, having a skill someone needs is power. But if no one needs our skills, "it is like having a disease for which there is nor cure." Powerlessness chips away at self-esteem and hinders personal growth.

Finally, the unrest, despair, and bitterness that go with unemployment can begin to be expressed in destructive behavior: increases in the rate of suicide, street crime, abuse in the family, and abuse of alcohol and other drugs. The stress of being without work and without hope of securing employment can result in physical illness. Is there anything else you would add to this experience?

Individual Caring Responses

In light of these strong feelings and experiences, what kinds of tangible and significant responses might caring Christians make? The following list is meant to be suggestive and not exhaustive. Add to it out of your group discussion.

Caring Christians will come to a better understanding of the experience of unemployment, including a careful examination of their own attitudes towards those who are without work.

Seek out person who are unemployed, especially if you are friends. Listen carefully to them. Do not assume that you know their needs until you have struggled with them in their experience. Beware of pat answers and quick advice. It does not help to speak of improved unemployment rates to someone who cannot find a job. Offer unemployed workers your relationship, and through that relationship affirm them as persons of worth and value. Let them identify needs to which you might respond. Offer child care if that is appropriate. Embody the sense of special concern and acceptance that Jesus had for persons who had been pushed to the margins of society. Using your best speaking skills, there may be appropriate times to remind them of Jesus's special concern for the powerless, and his value of persons for who they were and not for what they could produce.

Congregational Caring Responses

Encourage your congregation to make caring responses. Some of the hurts of the unemployed are so great that the larger resources of a congregation are needed. The following list of possibilities is meant to be suggestive and not exhaustive.

Take the initiative to provide a support group for those who seek employment. Let it be open to the community. It will be a community of shared pain. The support group does not provide any magic answers to participants, but it is a place where persons accept and encourage one another, share each other's failures and provide a place for honest expression of feelings. It is a group from which one cannot be fired! A support group can utilize outside resources to help persons analyze their job skills, teach how to write resumés, how to interview for a job, and how do deal with rejection. Persons give one another tips on job opportunities and sometimes baby-sit for each other while looking for work. The support group responds to the feelings of alienation and loneliness.

While the church is not equipped to function as a job service agency, members of the congregation could be made aware of people who are looking for work and the skills they have. At least some part-time work might be available. The model of local congregations helping refugees find a home and work is one that might be utilized with unemployed persons as well.

Often the church is criticized for its short-term responses to people who hurt, but some persons in the current unemployment crisis face serious and immediate needs and have nowhere to turn. The church might provide food pantries for short-term and immediate food needs, make good clothing available, and possibly even open the church building so that unemployed who are homeless have a place to stay. The hospitality of persons is used by God as a channel for grace.

Congregations will want to concern themselves with long-term caring responses where some of the root causes of unemployment and economic stress are addressed.

Finally, local congregations will encourage persons facing economic stress to continue to worship, and to participate in meaningful events that are designed not to cost money. The congregation will encourage persons in their faith, and point to the source of all hope.

Conclusion

The task of caring persons and the community of faith in the midst of a loss of self-esteem, powerlessness, and anxiety, is to affirm persons as being more than their work. Their usefulness as persons, rather, lies in who they are in relationship to God and to all of the community of faith.

Session 7

CARING FOR PERSONS WHO ARE HOMEBOUND

Introduction

Visiting persons who are unable to leave their homes or are in nursing homes is one of the most common acts of caring you might do. It is the kind of visit that most children will make as their parents grow older, a visit that many children report as being difficult to make. Our own attitude toward aging will have an effect on how helpful we will be in making a caring visit.

Purposes of the Session

The purposes of this session are to:
- encourage participants to reflect upon their attitudes toward aging,
- identify some of the thoughts and feelings experienced by persons who are confined to their homes or institutions,
- explore some caring responses that might be made to persons who are homebound, and
- practice some skills in making a caring visit.

Attitudes Toward Aging

The following process will help you reflect on your attitudes toward aging:

In the space below, write some words or images you use when you describe older persons. Do not analyze or think about the validity of what you write. Simply note what immediately comes to mind.

Now do a brief analysis of your words and images. What do they say about your feelings and understanding of aging?

Be prepared to share with others in the group. You might want to make note of some of their reflections in the space below.

It is important to accept aging as a part of our life experience. When we do that, we will be better prepared to reach out in caring ways to aging persons around us.

The Experience of Growing Older

What is it like to grow old and not have the freedom and independence we once had? Do we only see problems? Are we caught in some of the myths and stereotypes of growing old?

What is going on in the lives of persons who have lost some of their independence and mobility? What do they think? What do they feel? Rely on some of your own experience with older persons as you make your list.

Make a note of some of the insights shared by other members of your group.

Visiting the Person Who is Homebound

Once you have identified some of what persons who are shut-in think and feel, you are better prepared to make a caring visit.

Use the brief case study about Ruth that follows, or better yet, describe a person someone in your group knows. Try to imagine what Ruth or the person who was described might be experiencing. Determine some caring responses you as a new friend might make if you visited her.

Case Study of Ruth

Ruth was a stranger to the community and to everyone in the retirement home. She came with an "I don't like anything about this place" attitude. In that unhappy state she grumbled about the food, found fault with other residents, the nurses, and the administration, and complained that her children never visited her. Besides being lonesome, she had diabetes and failing eyesight.

What are some of the things that Ruth might be thinking and feeling?

What might be some caring responses that you could make? Be as specific as possible.

In the space below, make notes of some of the ideas from other members of your group.

The Reading Resource suggests some types of caring responses that can be made to persons who are shut-in.

Closing Worship

Read Psalm 92:12-15.

In prayer, reflect on your own attitude toward aging. Pray for a specific person who is shut-in. Consider making a commitment to visit the one for whom you pray.

THE EXPERIENCE OF BEING AN OLDER PERSON WHO IS HOMEBOUND

Introduction

One needs to be careful not to add to some of the stereotypes we already have of older persons in our society. Ageism is probably as pervasive as racism and sexism. One of the common myths about aging is that most older people become senile and are mentally inferior. Yet research reminds us that the average person's intelligence does not decrease as the person ages. The ability to think and reason can increase if the mind is exercised. The apparent loss of intelligence may be from constant put-downs, boredom, or just plain exasperation. Another common myth is that older people are all alike. The fact is that older persons actually become more diverse rather than more similar with advancing years. So we need to be careful not to assume that what is true for one older person will be true for another. Yet there are some experiences in aging that are common enough so that we might learn from them.

Reminiscence

Many older persons like to talk about the "good old days." Sometimes there is a repetition of stories. One form of loneliness among older persons, especially those who are in institutions, is that they have no one with whom to share common memories.

Reminiscence is an important and very natural process for all ages. It is not living in the past so much as living out of the past. It is a process of life review. It is a way to affirm oneself, to learn from one another, and to receive from each other.

A caring response to those who reminisce is to encourage persons to recall. Let them be our prophets. We might say, "I would like to hear you tell about those days." If we know persons well, we can encourage them to relive those experiences most meaningful to them. "Do you remember when...?" You might want to record some of these stories on cassette recorders, especially for the family or for church history. Use your best listening skills. An important understanding of God's grace is that we are valued for who we are, not for what we do.

Loneliness

There are many sources of loneliness for older persons in our society, not the least of which is the tendency for our culture as a whole to push older persons out of the mainstream of activities. Ours is a youth culture that tries to hide aging from our eyes and feelings. Other sources of loneliness might be due to the death of a spouse, geographical distance from family and close friends, psychological distance due to cultural and lifestyle differences, pain, or simply the lack of meaningful physical touch. Many of the elderly who experience loneliness become bitter.

Caring responses to those who are lonely will begin, not so much with, "How can I help this person?" as with "How can I create some space where this person can be listened to and responded to with careful attention?" There are ways to say, "I am here to be with you." Plan for an unhurried visit. Sit down near the one you are visiting. Relax! There may be times when you might arrange for children to have short visits. But remember, older persons are twice blessed by the visits of children: once when they arrive and once when they leave!

While you will want to be sensitive to individual differences in the desire to be touched, most older persons are hungry for meaningful physical touch. In his ministry, Jesus expressed concern for and healed people with a touch. A warm touch, a gentle stroke, or a carefully held hand can meet the hunger a person might feel to be in touch with another. If you say you will return for another visit, be sure to do so. In between times you might "reach out and touch" through a phone call.

A Sense of Loss

Persons who are shut-in and those who live in institutions will often experience a variety of losses: loss of physical health, including the loss of sight, hearing, and taste; the loss of psychological health, sometimes causing fears; some depression if their sense of well-being has been based upon health; and a loss of memory. If persons live in institutions, one must add the loss of the home where there has probably been a great deal of emotional investment; the loss of belongings, many of which are related to important life experiences; the loss of identity, especially if the new residence is in a different community; the loss of friends; the loss of privacy, space, and territory; and often a sense of loss of control, choice, and decision-making for oneself.

Caring responses will include some very practical actions. Always state who you are rather than ask, "Do you remember me?" Sit close at eye level, rather than hover over a person. If there is hearing impairment, it is best to speak slowly, use a little lower pitch in your voice, face the one to whom you are speaking, and use shorter sentences. It does not help to shout! Bring larger print materials or bring recorded material if eyesight is a problem. You might want to

bring a cassette tape of the worship service from the shut-in's church. Sit and listen with him or her. Visit about what you heard. Be prepared to ask if there is anything you might do, such as fix her/his hair, write a letter, run an errand, or provide transportation to see the doctor. It is possible that regular, volunteer contact with persons who are shut-in in their homes would enable them to remain in their homes for a longer period of time. A local congregation might organize and support such a caring ministry.

A caring response will include the use of your best listening skills. Encourage persons to express what they feel. There might be anger. They may want to talk about death. If you listen carefully and allow persons to express what they are feeling, more than likely you will be a ray of hope to help them rise above their losses. They may enter into some creative mental activities with you. You can help them reflect upon the resources of faith in their struggle over their losses and over the possibility of death itself. Above all, you will be invited to establish a meaningful relationship to replace some of the loss of relationships that they have experienced.

Decrease in Mental Functioning

Senility is not as great a problem among older persons as is sometimes perceived by younger persons. A large number of older persons pursue new ideas, keep up with current events and participate in or desire educational experiences. However, you will probably experience some decrease in mental functioning among some of the older persons you visit. Some of that senility is organic. That is, it has some physiological basis. Some senility is non-organic in that it is related to lack of stimulation.

Caring responses to persons with a decrease in mental functioning will include the use of "reality orientation." When there is confusion, it is more helpful to gently remind persons where they are, what time of year it is, and what some of their current relationships are. It is a good idea to check out information that is shared with you, such as, "My children never visit me," or "They never give me enough food here." Sometimes there may be a basis to what they say, while at other times it may be confusion. Speak in a calm and friendly manner. Do not speak to confused persons as if they were children. Give them a chance to reply; if they do not reply, you many want to rephrase your original statement.

Encourage stimulation through conversation and activities as much as possible. Involve older persons in decisions that are being made about their own lives. Read familiar passages of Scripture and pray the Lord's Prayer.

Summary

We have touched on some of what a homebound person might be experiencing, but not everything. As indicated earlier, older persons, especially those who are shut-in, face complex experiences. They will have feelings surrounding finances, sexuality, and in some locations, fear of crime. You are encouraged to do more reading in order to understand the aging process better.

While the emphasis in this session has been upon individual caring, there are times when larger caring issues need to be addressed by the whole community of faith. Financial resources, advocacy around housing and crime, education for all ages regarding the aging process, and stimulating educational experiences for older persons are some caring responses a congregation might make.

ILLNESS AND CARING

Introduction

Caring for the sick has always been a central concern for the people of God. An emphasis in the ministry of Jesus was to heal the sick, give sight to the blind, and to help the lame walk (Luke 4:18). It is the belief of Christians that God's healing powers come through people who genuinely care for one another.

Visitation of the sick will often be done in the hospital. However, there is a growing need to visit people in their homes because of shorter hospital stays and outpatient treatment, including outpatient surgery.

The basic purpose of the hospital or home visit is to be a channel through which God's love can be communicated to one who is ill. If that purpose is accomplished, those who are sick will feel understood, accepted, cared for; they will catch a ray of hope, and experience growth toward wholeness.

The Purposes of the Session

The purposes of this session are to:
- increase the participants sensitivity to the experiences and feelings of people when they are hospitalized or seriously ill at home,
- discuss some of the more helpful and less helpful things caring people do or say to persons who are ill, and
- practice using new insights for visiting persons in the hospital.

The Experience of Being Hospitalized

When persons are in the hospital, they may be in a crisis, or at the very least in a situation that produces anxiety. While hospitalized, most people do not always act or talk as they normally would.

If you have ever been hospitalized or close to one who has been in the hospital, try to recall the experience. It may be helpful to close your eyes. Recall the time and the place. What was the room like? Why were you there? Do you remember some of the feelings you had?

Who were some of the people around you? Recall some of the helpful things they did for you or said to you.

Recall some of the things that people did for you or said to you that were not helpful.

The Reading Resource, *Making a Caring Visit to the Sick*, has additional insights on being a caring person to those who are ill.

Visiting a Person Who is Hospitalized — A Role Play

The leader of the group will give you instructions for the role play. Record any new insights you gain from the discussion following the role play.

If you are in a small group of two or three people, you may want to talk about a specific person who is hospitalized. Describe the person and the situation as you know it. Using your insights and the Reading Resource, you could discuss some helpful things you might do or say in a visit.

Closing Worship

Read Luke 4:38-40 or 6:6-10.

Pray for specific persons who are ill. Pray for the healing of deep emotional wounds, for physical healing, and for growth toward wholeness.

You might touch one another as an expression of love and concern for the wholeness of each person in your group.

A READING RESOURCE

MAKING A CARING VISIT TO THE SICK

The Purpose of the Visit

BEFORE VISITING

There are some very practical things to consider before you make a visit. Plan to visit only when you are well yourself and during visiting hours. Think about making a phone call if a visit is not wise or possible.

Reflect for a few moments about what the person might be feeling. For example, the seriousness of surgery has little relationship to how it is viewed by the sick person. Fear or anxiety is often a pre-surgery mood. A visit the night before the surgery may be of great benefit. A sense of loneliness often follows a time of surgery. Since it is usually best to wait until the third day after surgery, you might send a card or note to arrive in those lonely times. If recovery is slow, depression is often experienced. Your visit might especially be appreciated at that time.

In any hospital experience, persons report feelings of vulnerability, which grow out of being in a strange environment, receiving orders from someone else, and not even having one's own clothes.

If the person is terminally ill, it will be especially helpful to be aware of some of the feelings that are being experienced. At least five different emotions are usually expressed. It is important to remember that people do not move through these emotions in nice, neat stages. The emotions are experienced with different intensities for varying lengths of time. One does not experience one emotion, complete it and move on. The feelings will return again and again.

It would be easier not to visit one who is terminally ill, yet it is in the midst of dying that we have one of the most significant opportunities for caring. An understanding of what the dying person and his or her family are experiencing can help us be more effective and less anxious caregivers.

Terminally ill persons will express denial or disbelief about a diagnosis. It grows out of shock and out of their inability to think of their own death for any lengthy period of time. Denial is usually a temporary defense against the thought of a person's own death.

There will be times of anger, often directed toward loved ones. It is usually safer to be angry at family or even at God.

Bargaining is the description given for terminally ill persons who want to postpone death by making promises to do or to be better than in the past. It is another way to cope with a difficult situation.

There are times of depression. Some of the depression is related to losses that have already occurred, such as bodily functions, job, or excessive costs of care. Some depression is related to the losses that are yet to come, such as close relationships and life itself.

Acceptance is an emotion expressed by terminally ill persons, too. It is a time of reflection and possibly even quiet expectation. Persons often misinterpret this as a time of giving up. The critically ill person is really preparing for the final break with people and life. Henri J. M. Nouwen said, in *In Memoriam*, that his mother thought and talked about her children until toward the end of her days she turned her eyes inward to see other realities.[2]

We will generally be more helpful caregivers if we spend a few moment thinking about what a person might be feeling. However, do not spend so much time identifying a certain step that you miss the person's deep needs and concerns. Use your best listening skills to determine what in fact is being experienced by the person you are visiting.

DURING THE VISIT

A quiet, calm manner is best when you enter the room, avoiding the overly cheery approach on the one hand or an extremely serious manner on the other.

Learn to evaluate the situation with a quick glance. Tubes, bottles, machines, cards and flowers (or lack of them), a rumpled bed, and especially facial expressions will tell you a lot about what is happening.

Make your opening greeting natural, based on your relationship. Say something like, "I'm sorry you are not feeling well" or "I wanted to stop by to see how you are doing;" then listen.

Illness often creates a sense of isolation. Touch can often help overcome the feeling of isolation. Touch communicates empathy, strength, and companionship, so do not be afraid of it. Touch is especially important when you visit terminally ill persons who are depressed or who express acceptance of their situation. Touch gives the assurance to dying persons that they are not alone. It is usually best to let the person who is ill take the lead

---

[2] Nouwen, Henri J. M. *In Memoriam*. Notre Dame, Indiana: Ave Maria Press, 1980, p. 22.

in offering you his or her hand. Respond with the same pressure they use.

It will be important to remember that the same person can have a different attitude every time you visit. This is especially true of one who is terminally ill. An understanding of the pattern identified by Kubler-Ross can help us respond in a more caring way to varied emotions. For example, if you sense denial is at work, you will accept that as a part of shock. Encourage persons to talk about their diagnosis when they take the initiative to share it.

If a person seems angry, you will want to create an okay feeling about expressing it, even toward God. We do not have to come to God's aid or defense. If anger is directed toward you, do not take it personally. Help persons express their anger, and its power will be reduced.

If the terminally ill person seems to want to "bargain," it is helpful to encourage a review of his or her past and to accept any desires to make promises about being a better person. Remember, many of these promises are not kept when people return home. Do not try to hold them to promises made. It is better to help people think about living one day at a time.

When people experience depression, it is more difficult to visit. They are usually not interested in the world or community news. Encourage them to express any sorrow. Sit with them in silence. Touch, They may ask for prayer.

When a terminally ill person expresses acceptance of death, it is usually best for other than intimate friends to give their attention to the family. They often need more help and support than the dying person.

Your visit will be more helpful if you are sensitive to what a person might be experiencing. Careful listening and looking will give you clues.

Be especially sensitive to the person's need to be left alone. If you detect pain, tiredness, or the need to use the bathroom, help the person get rid of you by saying, "I sense you are having some pain (or seem weary), so I would like to come back another time when it is more convenient." Sometimes we can communicate more love by leaving then we can by staying. Normally, visits should only be five to ten minutes in length. If someone would like to have you stay longer, he or she will usually let you know.

LEAVE-TAKING

When you prepare to leave, you might ask if there is anything you can get or do for the person. You may have identified something specific you can do from your conversation. Ask only if you are ready to respond to a request. The person might ask that you pray with them, read the Bible to them, make a telephone call, or run an errand.

One person reported that one of the most helpful good-byes he experienced while hospitalized was from a close friend who took his hand, held it tenderly, and simply said, "God is with you."

Keep in mind the possibility of visiting a person once he or she has left the hospital. Recovery at home can often be a lonely experience. During this time when many persons feel isolated, a caring visit might be greatly appreciated and provide for further healing.

Conclusion

It is quite clear that Jesus saw ministering to the sick as a way to communicate the love of God. Your caring visit made in a spirit of love, using good listening and speaking skills, and with sensitivity to what a person is experiencing, may become a channel through which God's love is still communicated. "Truly I say to you, inasmuch as you did it unto one of the least of these, you did it to me" (Matthew 25:40).

CARING FOR PERSONS LIVING WITH HIV/AIDS
by Bishop Fritz Mutti

Introduction

The number of persons infected with HIV, the virus that causes Acquired Immune Deficiency Syndrome (AIDS), increases each day. Hundreds of persons die weekly from causes related to this universally terminal illness.

In the future, every community will see some of its members affected by this devastating illness. For this reason every place urgently needs a large number of persons with the skills needed to care for those who suffer from the illness, and for their loved ones. Those who learn these skills of compassionate caring give a wonderful gift.

Purposes of the Session

The purposes of this session are to:
- provide participants with some needed basic information about HIV/AIDS,
- create a list of possible caring responses, and
- practice some skills in making a caring visit to someone living with AIDS.

AIDS 101

The first cases of Acquired Immune Deficiency Syndrome (AIDS) appeared in the United States in 1981. In a few months, medical professionals were reporting a disease of epidemic proportions. A huge wave of fear spread around the world, making it difficult to discuss a response.

Because many of those infected in the early months were gay men, an easy scapegoat was targeted. Medical misinformation circulated that only homosexual men were at risk. Theological misinformation accompanied this conclusion, claiming that God was judging homosexuality by causing these men to become ill.

Then it was discovered there was a high incidence of HIV/AIDS among intravenous drug users. A similar judgment arose. These persons were added to the list of scapegoats.

This did not reduce the fearfulness nor the condemnation. Persons were fired from their jobs and denied medical insurance. They were rejected by their families and ostracized by organizations throughout the community.

Gradually more knowledge of the virus causing AIDS was uncovered, and the medical community began to mobilize against the epidemic.

As a participant in this skill training for caregivers, you may have opportunity to visit someone living with HIV/AIDS. In the space below you may write answers to the questions as your leader states them.

Your local health department or Red Cross chapter has available several informational pieces about HIV/AIDS. In order to become more informed, you may want to secure some of these resources for study.

What is it Like to Live with AIDS?

In the space below, make a floor plan of your own work place. Sketch in the furniture and then draw a circle for each person who works near you. Now imagine that you are a person living with AIDS. How would your colleagues respond if they knew of your illness? Create symbols between you and the others which would indicate what you might expect from them. A broken line might indicate rejection. A heart might show compassion.

In your session, you will meet a person who is living with HIV/AIDS or see a video that helps you grow in understanding. As you listen to the presentation, take notes that will help you identify possible caring responses you might make.

Closing Worship

The Leader's Guide suggests a useful resource, entitled *Worship Resources for HIV & AIDS Ministries*. If that booklet is available, it may be used to plan a closing worship experience. If the booklet is not available, you might use the following:

- Read Isaiah 40:28-31 and Matthew 8:1-13

- Pray this prayer as a group:

"Many in our world are infected with HIV, O Creator God. In some countries nearly one-half of the population is HIV positive. Hear our prayer for these your people. Hear us as we pray for all those persons whose names we do not know and whose faces we would not recognize. Give insight to researchers who seek a vaccine or a cure. Guide physicians and nurses who administer treatment as effectively as they can.

And hear our prayer, O Loving God, for those infected whom we do not know. We pray for (names).... We ask You to be with them as comforter and sustainer. Lift them up and strengthen them every day. Take away their pain and give them hope.

Now make caregivers of us, O serving God. Grant us the gift of compassion, the willingness to touch, and the love to reach out.

We pray in the name of the One who came to heal the sick, Jesus Christ, our Lord. Amen."

A READING RESOURCE

CARING RESPONSES TO PERSONS LIVING WITH HIV/AIDS

Introduction

Because HIV/AIDS is a terminal illness, both those who are infected and those who seek to provide support and care will find it difficult to remain hopeful. Indeed the first response of one who learns of an HIV positive blood test result may well be, "I am going to die." Loved ones may find that is their first response as well. It is important to remember that it can take up to 10 years for HIV to become full-blown AIDS.

Amazingly, it is possible to move from such despair to hope. At the heart of the Christian Gospel is a witness to Jesus Christ. He was born into the world of sorrows and woes. He took on human flesh and experienced life as all persons experience it. Jesus was wrongly put to death by a hateful mob. He suffered an unimaginable death on a cross and was buried in a tomb that had been reserved for someone else.

Then, God raised him to life! That victorious life is offered to all and manifested through faith. In this ministry for others, both the one who is ill and the caregiver can claim the promise. Together they can refuse to submit to AIDS and begin living with AIDS.

Openness and Support

Caregivers can help create open, supportive, non-judgmental communities where people will feel safe to express their needs and ask for help. They may invite their congregations to enter a covenant to care. One church body provides this model covenant:

...we covenant together to assure ministries and other services to persons with AIDS. We ask for God's guidance that we might respond in ways that bear witness always to Jesus' own compassionate ministry of healing and reconciliation; and that to this end we might love one another and care for one another with the same unmeasured and unconditional love that Jesus embodied.[3]

They can encourage their congregations to state this covenant clearly and obviously. The pastor may mention during a worship service: "If you have AIDS, or are the loved one of a person who has AIDS, you are welcome here." The covenant can be posted on bulletin boards inside the church and noted on outdoor bulletin boards as well. An open congregation can provide a healing balm for many who suffer.

Anger

Persons living with HIV/AIDS may experience hostility and rejection that other terminally ill persons do not encounter. So while it is natural for everyone who is seriously ill to be angry about what is happening to them, persons living with HIV/AIDS may have to endure a large number of injustices as well.

With this illness there is an enormous amount of judgment. The victim is blamed over and over again by a frightened

---

[3] From "Resolution on AIDS and The Healing Ministry of the Church." *1992 Book of Resolutions*. Nashville: United Methodist Church, 1992.

community. Others pour hatred on those who are sick. Recipients of this hostility will surely have a great deal of anger about what is happening to them.

Caregivers can help a sick friend surface and release that anger. Moreover, they can stand with those being condemned and receive some of that hostility themselves. Such solidarity will have a healing and strengthening effect for the one who is ill.

Emotional Roller Coaster

Prepare yourself for huge swings in the well-being of the person you visit regularly. Persons living with AIDS may be desperately ill for several days and then relatively well for several months.

Gradually, however, as the immune system becomes more and more compromised, the opportunistic infections will occur more frequently. The one who is ill may be on the verge of death several times. Right before your eyes the body will waste away.

There is no way to avoid heart-rending emotional pain. You will ache in solidarity with the one you visit. What the person enduring such suffering needs from you, is a steady strength, a sense of hope, and a readiness to offer encouragement. You may want to work with the one you visit to enlist several persons who will provide a supportive network that will be available at all times.

Mobilize Resources

Caregivers who make available the resources of the faith community provide a wonderful service for the person who is ill. Here are some things that you can do:

- Offer prayer sometime during every visit, and include the one you visit in the church prayer chain.

- Read the scriptures. Many of the Psalms are appropriate. You might want to read through one of the Gospels over a period of several visits.

- Go to worship together.

- Ask your pastor to offer Holy Communion regularly.

Your congregation may give assistance, too. One Sunday school class took an offering each month and offered to help cover the cost of air fare for loved ones. A men's group recruited a lawyer to assist with legal matters. There are many other ways for the congregations to assist.

Identifying resources within the community can also be helpful.

- Find out what help is available from the Red Cross.

- See if there is a meals-on-wheels service.

- Discover who coordinates the "buddy" system. Buddies may come to visit regularly, do the grocery shopping, take care of the laundry, run errands. As a caregiver, you are a "buddy" in many ways.

- Arrange for transportation to and from the doctor or the hospital.

- Learn all you can about home-health care services.

Conclusion

Caregivers who visit persons living with AIDS need to stay with this ministry until the end. The sufferer will not be helped if caregivers cannot stay with them through the hardest times.

Planning for that time when death comes can be an enriching experience for all who are involved. Eventually the one who is ill must let go of life, and those who remain must cope with loss. Through it all, God will be an ever-present help and stay. All involved may offer this benediction:

Now to him who is able to keep you from falling, and to make you stand without blemish in the presence of his glory with rejoicing, to the Only God our Savior, through Jesus Christ our Lord, be glory, majesty, power, and authority, before all time and now and forever. Amen. (Jude 3:24-25)

Session 10

BEREAVEMENT AND CARING

Introduction

The death of a loved one is a jarring experience. Whenever death occurs, there is always pain in parting. If death is unexpected or at a young age, our sensibilities are attacked and what has always seemed sure is not so sure anymore. The amount of hurt we feel is related to how closely the fabric of life was woven together before the tear occurred.

The time of bereavement is a time for sensitive caring. The opportunity for this caring has come and will come to each one of us.

Purposes of the Session

The purposes of this session are to:
- help participants identify some of the feelings and experiences of persons who have lost a loved one through death,
- explore some possible caring responses to grieving persons,
- develop an awareness of less-than-helpful responses that are often made to bereaved people, and
- practice making a visit using insights on bereavement.

The Experience of Bereavement

An important resource for learning in this Session is the experience of the members of the group.

Recall a bereavement experience you have had. It may be loss through death of a close family member or a close friend. Describe the experience briefly.

Caring Responses to Bereaved Persons

List some of the things you felt and experienced during your bereavement.

Note some of the things other persons in the group experienced.

List some of the things people said or did that were helpful to you.

Record other insights from members of the group.

Write some of the things people said or did that were not helpful to you.

Record other insights from members of the group.

Read the Reading Resource to review these ideas and to gain new insights into bereavement and possible caring responses to grieving persons.

Making a Caring Visit

The leaders will give directions for a caring visit. This will not be a role play. You will be asked to visit about your bereavement with another person.

You may want to make a note of new insights that come from the discussion following the caring visit.

Closing Worship

Read Psalm 23 or 27.

Pray for the continued healing of your own grief, and pray for some specific person who is bereaved.

A READING RESOURCE

BEING A CARING PERSON TO ONE WHO IS BEREAVED

Introduction

Bereavement is probably the most common experience in life. It will visit everyone. Yet people are often at a loss about what to do or what to say for those who grieve. The anxiety about reaching out in less than helpful ways when bereavement comes may keep people from caring.

What might be some helpful responses caregivers can make to people who hurt so much? Caregivers should not think so much of stages of grief as in terms of tasks bereaved persons need to accomplish.

Be Available

One caring skill is that of availability. There is no better time to express that skill than at the time of death. We may not always know what to say, but we can be present. Many persons who experience loss by death report that they do not always remember what people said, but they do remember the people who called. They remember a touch or an embrace. Bereavement is first of all a time to hold hands with grief, not talk about it. Words will come later. People who grieve remember who brought food and helped to meet the needs of others who came to visit. They remember the people who ran errands and did some little jobs around the home. At the time of bereavement, caring people can be available.

Encourage the Expression of Emotions

Caring persons will encourage the expression of emotion that is obviously being felt. They will encourage bereaved persons to talk about the loss they have experienced. One's best listening skills will be utilized here. There is time for speaking later. It is especially important to refrain from pat answers to hard questions and the use of clichés to deeply felt emotions. It is okay for caring persons to "weep with those who weep." If people feel pain in their heart, it is more healing to help them express that, even if it is anger, than it is to keep it inside. It is not helpful to tell people to get hold of themselves. If people feel bitterness toward God, the doctors, clergy, the hospital, or other family members, encourage them to talk about it. Do not be afraid of emotions. Grief seems to apportion itself out so that we are not completely buried in on hugh landslide. People have to work through painful feelings. The power of these feelings can gradually be reduced through the help of a caring person who will listen, understand, and accept.

Give Support in Times of Depression

Bereaved persons will often have times of depression and may even feel all alone. They may say something like, "My family, or God, doesn't understand." "No one has ever felt like me." "Let's be honest with one another. Some of us think about suicide." A caring person will not try to argue the bereaved person out of these feelings. Healing can take place when there is careful listening. The attitude of the caring person is, "You are not alone. I am here with you. God is here with us." Hurting people can draw a sense of strength from caregivers and from the belief that God is with us in the midst of depression. If deep depression continues persons may need help from professionals. Use your referral skills.

Understand About Mental and Physical Distress

Caring persons can also help bereaved people understand that a great loss can make them worry about their own mental health. You might even hear someone say, "I think I am losing my mind." "I can't remember anything." The caring person will not say, "That's nothing to worry about." It will be more helpful to acknowledge that the feeling is kind of scary. It is real. But it is also natural in the grieving process. Persons report that just knowing that worry over their mental state is natural, helped them cope better.

Caring persons will help people who have experienced a significant loss understand that there will be an impact on their physical body. They many not be able to swallow food or they may actually become ill. If physical symptoms seem debilitating, encourage persons to visit their doctor.

Help Persons Deal With Regret

A common feeling among bereaved persons is guilt. The reason for guilt, which is experienced at different levels of intensity, is simple. No one has lived such a good life or had such good relationships to others that they cannot think of something they could have said or done differently while the person was still alive. The guilt is real, but it is also normal. It needs to be expressed and not glossed over as if it were unimportant. It is critical to face up to pain, guilt, and anger or those feelings can immobilize persons for years and erupt at anytime.

Caring persons will encourage people to speak of the guilt they feel. Their attitude will always be one of forgiveness. They will use their best speaking skills to help connect the forgiveness of the gospel with the grieving person's experience of guilt. If caregivers have had a similar experience, they might share some of their own story of forgiveness.

Encourage Activity

After some time, bereaved persons may still find it difficult to return to activities that were once important to them. People even report difficulty in returning to worship or to activities at church.

Caring people will encourage activity and reinvolvement in life again. They will invite grieving persons to a special community event, to a restaurant, or to their home. They will encourage the development of new relationships.

This may also be a time to encourage persons to read. Material that has been helpful in one's journey might be shared. Tell why it was meaningful. Reading materials should not be shared too early, for persons may still be living at an emotional level. Reading is a mental exercise that helps persons begin to make sense out of what has happened, to grow toward wholeness through new insights, and to gain some strength to re-engage more fully in life. Communicate that God offers new life and new challenges now.

Continue to Visit

Persons who have experienced loss often comment on how so many people were around and supported them for a week or two. Then they felt alone during the months that followed. Friends will continue to be sensitive to a person's loss and to make some special contacts for possibly a year. They will be aware that holidays, birthdays, special occasions, and the anniversary of the death are especially tender and difficult times for the bereaved person.

When visits are made, caregivers will talk about the person who has died. Some persons who have experienced loss begin to wonder if their loved one's life meant anything to anyone. Caring people will encourage remembrance by recalling some pleasant experiences or memories of the one who is dead. It is important to carefully choose the time to remember. It should be when there is time to be with each other and where tears will not be an embarrassment. Pray with grieving people. God is there with you.

Conclusion

All persons experience bereavement in different ways. For some, the impact of grief may last for a few days, for many it will last six months to two years, and for others it may last several years. The remembrance of the person and a sense of the loss that was incurred will probably never be forgotten.

What is needed in the most critical time of the bereavement, and what helps bereaved people most effectively, is the presence, caring, affection, and encouragement of other people. As this kind of support is given by caring people, it becomes easier to believe that life can be meaningful again. Bereaved persons will never be the same again, but with the help of caring people they can be more mature in their faith and gain strength to face the difficult moments in life. "We grieve, but not as those who have no hope." (I Thessalonians 4:13).

One of the beautiful things to observe and to encourage is that of bereaved persons coming to the place where they can reach out to others who have experienced loss. These "wounded healers" know what it means to be embraced, to be affirmed, and to be reminded of the presence of the Source of all caring — the God whom all can know and experience through the living Christ.

ADAPTING CARING SKILLS

Introduction

There are opportunities for caring that have not been addressed in these training sessions. People hurt in unique and special ways that we cannot always anticipate, but for whom we are called to care.

We have explored a variety of caring skills:
— good listening,
— careful speaking,
— availability,
— the ability to understand some of a person's experiences,
— and the process of making a caring visit.

Purposes of This Session

The purposes of this session are to:
■ illustrate the use of caring skills in a variety of situations where persons hurt,
■ experience the use of caring skills in a different kind of situation,
■ evaluate the *Ministry of Caring* training course, and
■ provide the opportunity for participants to dedicate themselves to a more intentional ministry of caring.

Identifying a Special Caring Opportunity

Identify a person for whom you have special concern, but whose particular kind of hurt or loss has not been addressed in this training experience; i.e., loneliness, teenage pregnancy, domestic abuse, or difficulty with the law. Briefly describe the person and the hurt or loss.

What do you sense that person is feeling or experiencing? List as many things as you can.

Possible Caring Responses

What are some of the things that people said or did that were helpful?

What are some of the things that people said or did that were less than helpful?

Adapting Caring Skills — A Role Play

Record any reflections that grew out of the group discussion after the role play.

Evaluation

The leader will give you instructions for any evaluation. One form of evaluation is provided in this Workbook on the following page.

Closing Worship

You are encouraged to plan for Holy Communion as a way to celebrate your time together. The Lord's Supper is a visible reminder of the community of caring to which we are called, and a resource to sustain us in our ministry together.

One hymn that might be used in closing is, "Blest Be the Tie That Binds."

EVALUATION OF *MINISTRY OF CARING* TRAINING

I felt best about:

The least helpful thing was:

	10	9	8	7	6	5	4	3	2	1	0
Setting	Appropriate										Inappropriate

	10	9	8	7	6	5	4	3	2	1	0
Activities	Appropriate										Inappropriate

	10	9	8	7	6	5	4	3	2	1	0
Directions	Clear										Unclear

	10	9	8	7	6	5	4	3	2	1	0
Participation	High										Low

The training might have been improved by (be specific):

My main learnings were:

I plan to be more intentional in caregiving by:

❑ I would be available to visit with another whose need is:

(Please sign) ⎯⎯⎯⎯⎯⎯⎯⎯⎯⎯⎯⎯⎯⎯⎯⎯⎯⎯⎯⎯⎯⎯

❑ I would like to be a part of a Ministry of Caring Support Group.

(Please sign) ⎯⎯⎯⎯⎯⎯⎯⎯⎯⎯⎯⎯⎯⎯⎯⎯⎯⎯⎯⎯⎯⎯

❑ I would like further training in the areas of:

and:

(Please sign)⎯⎯⎯⎯⎯⎯⎯⎯⎯⎯⎯⎯⎯⎯⎯⎯⎯⎯⎯⎯⎯⎯